At Home

Long Ago and Today

Lynnette R. Brent

Heinemann Library
Chicago, Illinois

Design by Herman Adler Design
Editorial Development by
Morrison BookWorks, LLC
Photo Research by Carol Parden,
Image Resources
Printed and bound in the United States by
Lake Book Manufacturing, Inc.

07 06 05 04
10 9 8 7 6 5 4 3 2

**Library of Congress Cataloging-in-
Publication Data**
Brent, Lynnette R., 1965-
At home: long ago and today /
Lynnette R. Brent.
    p. cm. -- (Times change)
Summary: An introduction to how houses and
their care have changed in the past one hundred
years, discussing materials used to build
homes, various ways to heat and cool them,
and how chores have changed over time.
Includes bibliographical references and index.
    ISBN 1-4034-4531-1 (Library Binding-hard-
cover) -- ISBN 1-4034-4537-0 (Paperback)

1. Dwellings--History--Juvenile literature.
2. Home economics--History--Juvenile literature.
[1. Dwellings--History. 2. Home economics--
History.] I. Title. II. Series.
    TX301.B64 2003
    690'.837'0973--dc21
                        2003011029

Acknowledgments
The author and publishers are grateful to
the following for permission to reproduce
copyright material: pp. 1(t), 6(b-r), 10(b),
30(b-m) Bettmann/Corbis, p. 1(b) Comstock
Klips; pp. 5, 14, 18(t-l) 22(both), 26, 30(b-l)
Brown Brothers; pp. 6(t),9, 10(m-l), 13, 16,
23, 24 Corbis; pp. 7, 19 Bob Daemmrich
Photography; p. 8 Museum of History &
Industry/Corbis; p. 11 Courtesy of Trane, a
business of American Standard Companies
Inc. ©2003; pp. 12, 28 Minnesota Historical
Society; p. 15 Fotografis/Corbis; p. 17 Carlos
Dominguez/Corbis; p. 18(b-r) Electrolux Home
Products; p. 20(t-l) Hulton-Deutsch
Collection/Corbis, pp. 20(b-r), 30(b-r) Maytag
Corporation; p. 21 Michael Newman/
PhotoEdit; p. 25 Ariel Skelley/Corbis;
p.27 Myrleen Ferguson Cate/PhotoEdit;
p. 29 Tony Freeman/PhotoEdit

Cover photographs reproduced with permission
of (t) Minnesota History Society, (b) Bob
Daemmrich Photography

Every effort has been made to contact
copyright holders of any material reproduced
in this book. Any omissions will be rectified
in subsequent printings if notice is given to
the publisher.

Some words are shown in bold, **like this.**
You can find out what they mean by looking
in the glossary.

Contents

Long Ago

Imagine that it is long ago. Your family is sitting in the parlor with friends on a Saturday night. Everyone is dressed nicely and having fun. Your sister begins to play the piano. Everyone joins her at the piano and begins to sing! It is such fun to spend the night with friends and family in your home.

This is what you may have been doing for fun at home if you lived 100 years ago. What other things would you do at home if you lived long ago? What would your home look like? Let's see what life was like at home long ago.

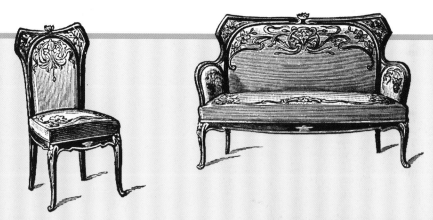

Long ago, families spent time in their parlors with friends.

Where Is Home?

Many people lived in farmhouses on their farms.

Long ago, most people lived on farms. Some of the people from the farms moved into cities. There were also people from other countries moving into the cities. Cities like New York City, Chicago, and Philadelphia became larger with all the people who were moving into them.

Times Change

What Changed in 1947?

In 1947, Levittown, New York was built by Alfred and William Levitt. Before Levittown, each home had its own design. In Levittown, each home had the same design. This meant the houses could be built and sold quickly.

Levittown changed the way houses were built forever.

This family lives in a suburb outside a large city.

Today, many people live in cities and towns.
Few people still live on farms. Many people also
live in **suburbs.** Suburbs are smaller cities that
surround large cities. Many of the people who
live in suburbs still work in the large city they are
close to. They drive or take the train to get to
work and back home each day.

Types of Homes

Long ago, homes were built by hand. Most families built their homes with wood and **mortar**. Mortar is a mixture of sand, water, and cement that hardens when it dries. Families would use mortar to hold the pieces of wood together. More expensive homes were made of brick. All homes took a long time to build.

Long ago, families built their own houses.

Today, machines help people build homes faster. Bulldozers, cranes, and many kinds of electric tools are some of the machines used to build homes. Homes are made of wood, brick, **stucco**, and **aluminum siding.** Today, people live in houses, apartments, mobile homes, or townhouses.

Today, construction workers use machines to build houses for other people.

Heating and Cooling the Home

Long ago, most homes did not have electricity. Most people burned wood in a fireplace or coal in a stove to keep warm. To keep cool, homes were built with big doors and windows. Some houses had porches where people sat on hot summer nights. Even with these things, homes did not stay very cool on hot days.

A porch was a great place to keep cool on hot days.

Times Change

What Changed in 1928?

In 1928, Willis Carrier developed the Weathermaker. It was the first air conditioner made just for people's homes. Before the Weathermaker, only stores and movie theaters had air conditioning. Carrier's air conditioner was a lot larger than the ones used today.

Willis Carrier developed the Weathermaker.

Air conditioners like this one keep homes cool on hot summer days.

Today, many homes have air conditioning. Air conditioning keeps homes cool on the hottest days. It has helped many people to be more comfortable in their homes. While some homes still have fireplaces, heat comes from electricity or gas. Stoves that burn coal are not used today for heat.

The Living Room

The parlor was a room used
when guests came to visit.

Long ago, people had a living room called a
parlor. It was near the front of the house and
used for many things. In the parlor, people
spent time talking and laughing. People also
played instruments and sang together. The
parlor was a great place to have fun.

Today, many people have living rooms instead of parlors. The living room is only one of many rooms people use today when they have guests visiting. Family rooms, basements, and kitchens are all rooms that can be used for fun today. All kinds of activities happen in these rooms when guests are visiting.

The living room is a place where families can spend time together.

The Bathroom

People used outhouses when they did not have bathrooms inside their homes.

Long ago, only families with a lot of money had bathrooms with running water. Bathrooms with running water had indoor toilets and bathtubs. Most families did not have indoor toilets or bathtubs. The toilet was outside in an outhouse. The bathtub was a metal tub that they filled up with water from a well or **faucet** in the backyard.

Today, almost all families have bathrooms with running water in their homes. Bathrooms have toilets, sinks, bathtubs, and showers. Sometimes bathtubs and showers are separate from each other. Some homes have only one bathroom. Others have as many bathrooms as they do bedrooms!

Most homes have bathrooms with toilets, bathtubs, and showers.

The Bedroom

Long ago, not all homes had bedrooms. Some homes had one large room for everyone to sleep in together. Some homes had one bedroom for the parents and one bedroom for all the children. Sometimes all the children slept in one bed. Children had beds, dressers, and only a few toys in their bedroom.

Sometimes families had one big room for sleeping and cooking!

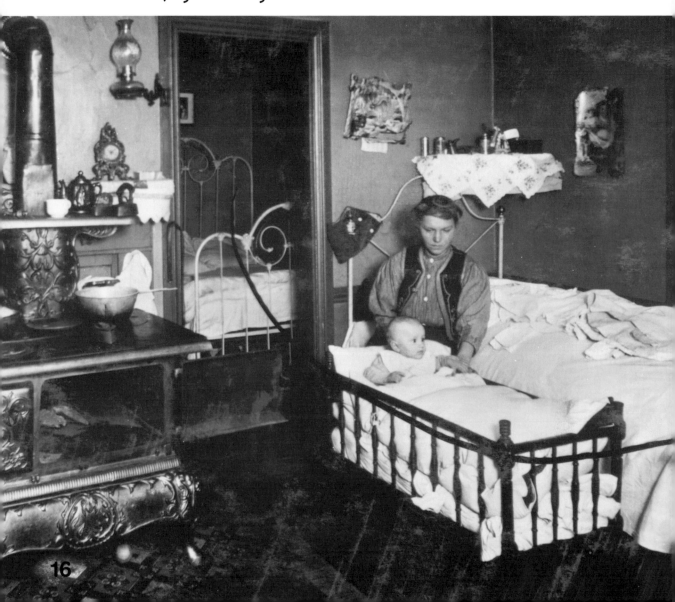

Today, many children have their own bedrooms where they sleep and play.

Today, most homes have at least two bedrooms. Parents still share one bedroom. Some children also share bedrooms. Most of the time brothers share with brothers, and sisters share with sisters. A few children have their own bedrooms. Children still have bedrooms with beds and dressers, but today they keep more toys in the bedroom.

The Kitchen

Long ago, women spent many hours in the kitchen cooking dinner for their families.

Long ago, kitchens were used mostly for cooking food. Women used fireplaces or stoves to cook food on. There were no refrigerators. Some kitchens had an icebox, a cabinet that held ice to keep food cool and fresh. Most kitchens long ago did not have running water. Instead, people brought water into the house from a well or **faucet** in the backyard.

Times Change

What Changed in 1915?

In 1915, the first refrigerator for the home was developed. It was called the Guardian, and was built in Fort Wayne, Indiana.

The refrigerator was an important invention for the kitchen.

Today, kitchens are used for cooking and many other things. Many kitchens still have ovens and stoves to cook food. Most kitchens have running water and refrigerators to keep food fresh and cool. Some children like to do their homework there. The kitchen is a place where families and friends gather to be social.

Families today spend less time cooking and more time socializing in the kitchen.

What's for Dinner?

Families could get some foods only during certain times of the year.

Long ago, families could eat foods that were only available during a certain season. Families that lived in cities got much of their food from the store. They ate foods like bread, meat, and canned foods. Families that lived in the country grew or hunted their food. They ate cornmeal mush, bacon, and fish.

Times Change

What Changed in 1967?

In 1967, the first microwave oven for the home, the Radarange, was sold. Before then, it took people a long time to get dinner ready. The Radarange was very expensive, and few people could afford it.

The Radarange let people cook dinner in less time.

20

Today, grocery stores and refrigerators help keep foods fresh all year long. Families can eat fruits and vegetables in the summer and in the winter. People in cities and the country eat many of the same things.

Today, families have many choices of what to eat all year long.

Cleaning the Home

Long ago, cleaning the house took days! There were no electric machines to help people clean. Water from outside was brought in and boiled to wash clothes, dishes, and floors. People did not have soap from the store to help them do these jobs. They had to make their own soap.

Some people had hand-crank washing machines to help them wash their clothes.

Times Change

What Changed in 1905?

In 1905, the first portable vacuum cleaner was invented. It was called the Skinner Vacuum. Not many people bought it because it was so heavy. It took a few years for vacuum cleaners to become popular in the home.

The Skinner Vacuum was very large and weighed 92 pounds.

Today, machines that use electricity help people clean. People use vacuum cleaners to clean their rugs and carpets. Many people have washers and dryers to clean their clothes and dishwashers that clean their dishes. People do not have to make their own soap anymore. They buy cleaning products in stores.

Washing machines today work by electricity.

Working in the Home

Long ago, people worked inside and outside of the home. Most men worked outside the home in factories and offices. Women made money working at home. Some sewed clothes or decorated hats. Farm families grew food and raised animals. They sold things like milk, eggs, and corn to make money.

To make more money, mothers often had their children help them sew clothes.

Today, some people run businesses from a home office.

Today, many people leave home to go to work, but some people still work in their homes. Many of these people have home offices. A home office is a place in a home where someone can run a business.

Some families today still own farms and sell things from their farm to make money.

Children's Chores Around the Home

On farms, many children fed the chickens as one of their chores.

Long ago, children had many kinds of chores to do. On farms, children milked cows, collected chicken eggs, and fed animals. Some boys chopped firewood and got water from the well. Others picked fruit and vegetables. Girls helped their mothers keep the house clean. They washed clothes, dishes, and floors.

Today, children's chores are much different. Most children do not have to milk cows or collect chicken eggs. Instead, they take care of pets. Some children help with setting the table before dinner or taking out the garbage. Others help outside by cutting grass, raking leaves, or shoveling snow. Children today have different chores than children did long ago.

One of this girl's chores is to feed her cat every day.

What's Outside the Home?

Long ago, people had stables instead of garages.

Long ago, few homes had garages because most people did not have cars. In 1900, there were only 8,000 cars in the United States! Instead, most people used horses, mules, or bicycles to get around. People kept horses, mules, and bicycles in stables.

Many homes had small yards in the front, side, or back of the house. Families used these yards to sit outside and relax.

Some garages are attached to the home.

Today, many houses have garages where people keep their cars. Most people don't have stables because they do not use horses or mules anymore. Many people still keep their bicycles in garages with the cars. Yards are still popular places to relax. Today, yards are bigger than long ago. Some yards may even have jungle gyms, swimming pools, or tennis courts!

Life at home has changed in the past 100 years! One hundred years ago, you may have slept in one big room with the rest of your family. You may have had to work a lot harder than you do today to keep your home warm and clean.

But some things about homes are the same. There are still yards to play in, places to eat and sleep, and places to be with family and visit with friends. Most importantly, houses of today and long ago both have families who call them "home."

Times Change

1905	**1915**	**1928**	**1947**	**1967**
The Skinner Vacuum is invented.	The first refrigerator for the home, the Guardian, is developed.	The first air conditioner for the home, the Weathermaker, is developed.	Levittown is founded in New York.	The Radarange microwave is developed for the home.

Radarange microwave

Skinner Vacuum

Levittown, New York

Glossary

aluminum siding outside covering of a house that is made of a light material

faucet tool connected to a sink that turns water on and off

mortar mixture of sand, cement, and water that hardens when it dries

stucco plaster used for covering walls

suburb district, town, or village just outside or near a city

More Books to Read

Gourley, Catherine. *Welcome to Samantha's World 1904: Growing Up in America's New Century.* Pleasant Company Publications. Middleton, WI, 1999.

Scott, Janine. *Life Long Ago.* Compass Point Books. Minneapolis, MN, 2002.

Ask an older reader to help you read this book:

Kalman, Bobbie. *The Victorian Home.* Crabtree Publishing, St. Catharines, Ontario, Canada, 1996.

Index